THE TALKING SCOTS QUIZ BOOK

WILLIAM GRAHAM, past chairman of the Scots Language Society and past president of Ayr Burns Club, lives in Alloway by the mill on the River Doon where Burns received his first schooling. Born in Carluke in 1913 and educated at Wishaw High School and Glasgow University, he has been teacher, nurseryman, organist and poet. In 1973 he won the £1000 first prize in a magazine story-writing competition, and left teaching to concentrate on the work nearest his heart, a 1600-page English-Scots Dictionary which was published in abridged form in 1977 as "The Scots Word Book." He also won first prize in the Scots Section of the Scottish Open Poetry Competition in 1977, and has been the question-setter for the popular S.T.V. "Talking Scots" series since its inception.

Other works by
WILLIAM GRAHAM

Scots Verse
"That Ye Inherit"
"Twa-Three Sangs and Stories"

Scots Language
"The Scots Word Book"

Cassette
Poetry Readings (Scotsoun)

the talking scots Quiz Book

Compiled by

WILLIAM GRAHAM

Alloway *Publishing*

AYR

© William Graham, 1981

First Published in 1981
by Alloway Publishing Ltd.,
High Street, Ayr.

Printed in Scotland
by Walker & Connell Ltd.,
Hastings Square, Darvel,
Ayrshire.

ISBN 0 907526 07 1

INTRODUCTION

It cannot be too often repeated that Scots is not simply a gutter form of English, but is a language in its own right — and an illustrious one at that.

So, while the intention in producing this book is primarily to provide a series of light-hearted quizzes for the ever-growing number of Burns clubs and others that are showing a renewed interest in their native speech, the hope is that it will also do its own small part in preserving the guid Scots tongue from complete extinction.

The questions are arranged in seven separate programmes, each containing a sufficient number of rounds on various topics to occupy a whole evening, or only part of an evening if some other activity is also intended. The programmes are equally suitable for either a "syndicate" quiz for companies of up to sixty or more people divided into teams of four, five, or six persons, or for two panels of three contestants each, or one panel of three contestants altogether. Thus the questions will be suitable for anything from a simple group of three people, to two opposing teams, say from two separate Burns clubs, or towns, or schools — or one large company of people divided into a number of opposing teams.

For a "syndicate" quiz, the following suggestions are made. A chairman will arrange the meeting into groups of four, five, or six people, and each group will be supplied with a sheet of paper and one of its members appointed to mark it with an identifying number which the chairman will give to each group, and to write down the group's agreed answer to each question.

On completing each round of questions, each group will hand its answers to a neighbouring group for marking — a tick or a cross for a right or a wrong answer — and totals for each round will then be taken in by the chairman and chalked on a blackboard by his assistant for all to see the "state of the parties."

The members of the winning group after the programme or agreed part of the programme is gone through may then be presented with small prizes. Alternatively, each of the first two winning groups may appoint a champion, who will then compete in a group of questions selected from the lists of questions appearing in the book after the seventh programme (pages 66 to 74).

On the other hand, the questions are set in groups of six (twelve in the case of the Quickies round), so that if only one panel of three, or two panels of six, persons are involved, the questions can be put directly to the panellists, all or only half according to circumstances, with an assistant to keep the scores prominently displayed on a blackboard for the audience's benefit.

CONTENTS

PROGRAMME ONE

ROUND ONE — Scots into English Quickies

Note: Three sets of twelve words each are given, these sets being arranged in order of difficulty. For a syndicate quiz, the chairman should choose A, B, or C according to his estimate of the company's knowledge of Scots words. In the case of a panel, it is suggested that each panellist might be asked to choose his/her set in advance, with one point only being awarded for correct answers in set A, two points in set B, and three points in set C.
Pronunciation is given where necessary in brackets.

Give the meaning of the following nouns or naming words:-

Set A	Set B	Set C
1. bawbee	1. cundy	1. cranreuch *(kranruch — guttural)*
2. airt	2. heuk *(hyuk or hyook)*	2. crawsteps
3. bauchle	3. hairst	3. harns
4. clout/cloot *(kloot)*	4. houlet *(hoolet)*	4. sarkin
5. breeks	5. graip *(grape)*	5. brecham *(guttural)*
6. joug *(joog)*	6. ingle *("ng" as in "sing")*	6. craig
7. kail	7. quaich *("ch" — guttural)*	7. trews
8. sheuch *(shuch — guttural, or shooch)*	8. rodden tree	8. swee
9. peenie	9. scaffie	9. awl
10. kist	10. shairn	10. maskin pot
11. tawse	11. dub	11. but-and-ben
12. lowe *(as in "now")*	12. mowdie	12. spigot

ROUND TWO — Mixter-Maxter

One point for each correct answer.

1. What would you be doing if you took part in a Scotch convoy?
2. What would a person mean who said, "I never saw the maik o thae parritch afore"?
3. If a boy took the dourles *(doorls)*, what would be wrong with him?
4. What would a person mean by referring to something as being cauld kail het again?
5. If someone took you ower the coals, what would he be doing?
6. If someone said he was gaun to chynge his feet, what would he be meaning?

ROUND THREE — True or False

Say whether the following statements are true or false.

One point for each correct answer. An extra point for an explanation.

1. A teuch *(tyuch)* jean was the name often given to a hard-bitten primary school teacher in the Glasgow area, who ruled her class with a rod of iron.
2. "Caw the yowes to the knowes" means, cry the ewes to come to the rising ground or the hillocks.
3. A whistle binkie was one who attended a "penny wedding" without paying, and so had to whistle and entertain the company.

4. "Caller oo!" was the cry set up by itinerant buyers travelling the country districts to collect the fresh season's wool for making into raploch, or course woollen cloth.
5. A claw hammer was an article of dress.
6. "Gaen *(gane)* aa to pigs an whussles" — in this phrase, the "pigs" part refers to the Bible story of the destruction of the Gadarene swine. The whussles reference is not known. So it means gone to destruction like the Gadarene swine.

ROUND FOUR — How did Burns put it?

The following are prose translations, each of two lines of a Burns poem.

One point given for each line correctly quoted, and one point for the name of the poem from which lines are taken. Three points in all.

1. When itinerary salesmen forsake the street, and people needing a drink meet up with each other . . .
2. They are bullocks when they enter (college) and asses when they leave it, if the truth be told.
3. But yet, Lord, I must admit that I'm sometimes bothered with the demands of the flesh.
4. When leaves of variegated colours cover the ground, or flickering in the air like the bat . . .
5. Old Scotland does not want any watery soup that splashes in bowls.
6. Would that we might be given the ability to look upon ourselves as others find us to be!

ROUND FIVE — Christian Names

Give the English equivalents of the following.

One point for each correct answer.

1. Dandie
2. Buntie
3. Dod
4. Effie
5. Gibbie
6. Kirstie

ROUND SIX — How it's said in Scots

What do these expressions mean?

One point for each correct answer.

1. Auld claes and parritch.
2. Cowp somebody's hurly.
3. The heid bummer.
4. Tak something ill out *(oot)*.
5. It'll be the price o him.
6. No a steik *(steek)* to pit on.

ROUND SEVEN — What are they in Scots?

Give the Scots for the following objects.

One point for each correct answer.

1.

Child's metal hoop.

2.

Garden trowel.

3.

Scraper with long handle
for drawing clinkers out
of furnaces etc.

4.

Teacher's strap.

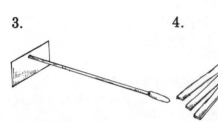

5.

Wooden box with long
handle passed along
pews for church collection.

6.

House slippers.

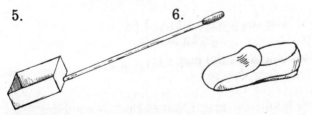

ROUND EIGHT — Quote Round

Supply the missing words for three points, and name
of poem from which the lines are taken for one point.

1. Bonnie — 's nou *(noo)* awa,
    Safety owre the friendly —;
    Monie a — will brek in twa,
    Should he ne'er come back again.

2. I'm — awa, John,
    Like snaw — in thaw, John;
    I'm — awa (same word as in first line)
    To the land o the —.

3. Why — ye by the tide, ladye,
    Why — ye by the tide, (same word as in first line).
    I'll wed ye to my — —,
    And ye sall be his bride.

4. "Ye'll sit on his white hause —,
    And I'll pyke out his bonnie — een;
    Wi ae lock of his gowden hair
    We'll — our nest when it growes bare."

5. O our Scots nobles were richt laith
    To — their cork-heeled shoon;
    But lang or aa the play were —,
    Their hats they swam —.

6. We'll hear nae mair lilting at the yowe milking,
    Women and bairns are heartless and —,
    Sighing and moaning on ilka green —,
    The — of the forest are aa wede away.

PROGRAMME TWO

ROUND ONE — Scots into English Quickies

Note: Three sets of twelve words each are given, these sets being arranged in order of difficulty. For a syndicate quiz, the chairman should choose A, B, or C according to his estimate of the company's knowledge of Scots words. In the case of a panel, it is suggested that each panellist might be asked to choose his/her set in advance, with one point only being awarded for correct answers in set A, two points in set B, and three points in set C.

Pronunciation is given where necessary in brackets.

Give the meaning of the following adjectives or descriptive words:-

Set A	Set B	Set C
1. tuim/toom	1. birky	1. canty
2. caurry-fistit *(corrie-)*	2. pernickety	2. dowie
3. peelie-wallie	3. diffie	3. eldritch
4. sleekit	4. sliddery	4. fremmit
5. sweirt *(sweert)*	5. mim-mou'd *(moo'd)*	5. haisert
6. wizzent	6. shilpit	6. careous *(kare-us)*
7. laich *("ch" — guttural)*	7. skeely	7. unco
8. blate	8. spirlie	8. nesh
9. bruckle	9. perjink	9. siccar
10. canny	10. douce *(dooss)*	10. slee
11. clarty	11. feckless	11. auld-farrant
12. heich *(heech — guttural)*	12. fozie	12. begrutten

ROUND TWO — Proverbs

Supply the missing words with the aid of clues for
two points, and give the meaning of the proverb for
one point. Each dash stands for a letter.

1. There's aye some w - - - r whaur the st - - kie
   drouns *(droons)*.
2. Guid - - - - gangs into wee - - - -.
3. He that gies aa his gear to his ba - - - s,
   Tak up a be - - le and ding out his harns.
4. A skelpit - - - braks nae ba - - s.
5. Eat the c - o and worry on the t - - l.
6. Dinna let the ban - - ts gae by w - - tin for the hats.

ROUND THREE — Burns Round

Supply the missing line for one point, and give the
name of the poem from which it is taken for another
point. Each dash stands for a word.

1. Now we maun totter doun, John,
   — — — — — —

2. Five rousty *(roosty)* teeth, forby a stump,
   — — — — — —

3. Till aa the seas gang dry, my dear,
   — — — — — —

4. And owsen frae the furrowed field
   — — — — —

5. Yestreen, when to the trembling string,
   — — — — — —

6. Caw them where the burnie rowes,
   — — —

ROUND FOUR — Food

What are the following?

One point for each correct answer.

1. Tatties-'n-dab
2. Coddled aipples
3. Sowens
4. Brose
5. Stovies
6. Skirl-i-the-pan

ROUND FIVE — True or False

Say whether the following statements are true or false.

One point for each correct answer. An extra point for an explanation.

1. A bumclock is a squat-shaped timepiece with an exceptionally large receptacle for its inner "works".
2. Dandelions in seed are called clocks in certain parts of the country.
3. A deoch-an-dorus (dyoch — guttural) is the Gaelic for a but-and-ben or two-apartment house.
4. Hunt-the-Gowk was an old custom by which the first lad to hear a genuine cuckoo call in spring was awarded a kiss by the bonniest lass in the village.
5. To chap in dominoes means you haven't got a suitable domino to play, so you miss your turn.

6. Riding the stang was a punishment meted out to
    adulterers and wife beaters.

ROUND SIX — How it's said in Scots

What do these expressions mean?

One point for each correct answer.

1. Weit *(weet)* The whussle.
2. Caw a bike.
3. The croun *(croon)* o the causey *(cawssie)*.
4. Stick up to.
5. A greetin Teenie.
6. Lappert milk.

ROUND SEVEN — Sentences for Translation

Translate the following sentences into English,
showing you know the meanings of the words and
phrases underlined, for three points.

1. <u>Speir</u> at a <u>keeking-gless</u> owre often, and ye'll see
    a <u>gowk</u> at the back o't.
2. I gied the auld <u>nipscart</u> a caa at his teatime, and
    he didna as muckle as say, <u>"Collie will ye lick"</u>.
3. Ye'll ne'er fin a <u>brammle worm</u> in a <u>midden</u> o
    <u>green dung.</u>
4. The <u>callan</u> 'll loss his <u>steerin</u> weys <u>or</u> he's muckle
    aulder.

5. Yon <u>donnert</u> wee <u>nyaff</u> 'll never <u>mak saut to his</u>
   <u>kail.</u>
6. She was a <u>girnin,</u> <u>carnaptious</u> auld <u>hizzy</u>.

ROUND EIGHT — Mixter-Maxter

One point for each correct answer.

How did they play the game of —

1. Stookies or Statues?
2. Kick the Can?
3. Buttony?
4. Lang Heidies?
5. Chuckies?
6. Peevers?

PROGRAMME THREE

ROUND ONE — Scots into English Quickies

Note: Three sets of twelve words each are given, these sets being arranged in order of difficulty. For a syndicate quiz, the chairman should choose A, B, or C according to his estimate of the company's knowledge of Scots words. In the case of a panel, it is suggested that each panellist might be asked to choose his/her set in advance, with one point only being awarded for correct answers in set A, two points in set B, and three points in set C.

Pronunciation is given where necessary in brackets.

Give the meaning of the following verbs or doing words:-

Set A	Set B	Set C
1. dicht ("ch" guttural)	1. wheeple	1. big
2. douk (dook)	2. birsle	2. scrieve (screeve)
3. drouk (drook)	3. plowter	3. sain
4. guddle	4. redd	4. handsel
5. jouk (jook)	5. taigle	5. dree
6. speir (speer)	6. tent	6. snicker
7. lowse (lowze)	7. theik (theek)	7. slorp
8. chitter	8. threip (threep)	8. soo
9. coorie	9. runkle	9. wale
10. argie-bargie	10. dwyne	10. yammer
11. greit (greet)	11. gar	11. yeuk
12. grumph	12. cowp	12. flicher

ROUND TWO — Proverbs

Supply the missing words with the aid of clues for two points, and give the meaning of the proverb for one point. Each dash stands for a letter.

1. A t - - - - - less (purseless) dame sits lang at h - - -.
2. Aft e - - le (attempt), wh - - - - (sometimes) hit.
3. Aye hae your c - g (bowl) out when it rains k - - l.
4. A wife is w - ce enough that kens her guidman's b - - - ks frae her ain kirtle.
5. Flee 1 - - ch, flee l - ng.
6. A f - - l and his s - - - - - 's easy pairtit.

ROUND THREE — Burns Round

The following lines from "Tam o' Shanter" have been deliberately misquoted. The wrong words are in italics. Give the correct version for three points.

1. The *beer* sae reamed in Tammie's *heid*,
   Fair play, he cared na deils a *faurthen*.
2. Ah! little kenned thy reverent *mammy*,
   That *shirt* she *bocht* for her wee nanny . . .
3. As Tammie *watched, bumbazed* and curious,
   The mirth and fun grew fast and *riotous* . . .
4. Even Satan glowered and *wriggled* fou *eagerly*,
   And hotched and *puffed* wi micht and main . . .
5. She tauld thee *often* thou wast a *rogue*,
   A *talkative*, blusterin, drunken blellum . . .
6. Ah, gentle *wives!* it *makes* me greit,
   To think how *often* counsels sweet . . .

ROUND FOUR — Sentences for Translation

Translate the following sentences into English, showing you know the meanings of the words and phrases underlined, for three points.

1. <u>It's no for</u> a <u>shilpit</u> wee body like her to be <u>stravaigin</u> aa ower the toun in siclike wather.
2. Ye <u>gormless</u> big <u>gomeril!</u> Ye should <u>think black burnin shame</u> o yoursel!
3. A <u>backgaun</u> bairn was said <u>langsyne</u> to hae gotten a <u>waff</u> o the ill ee.
4. Gin ye was <u>wyce,</u> ye wad <u>be for hame</u> or pub <u>skailin time.</u>
5. <u>Trowe</u> your <u>girr</u> wi your ain <u>cleik!</u>
6. I see <u>Auldhill's</u> <u>weel forrit</u> we his plouin <u>the year.</u>

ROUND FIVE — Christian Names

Give the English equivalents of the following.

One point for each correct answer.

1. Habbie
2. Beenie
3. Girzie
4. Lowrie
5. Leebie
6. Mirren

ROUND SIX — How it's said in Scots

What do these expressions mean?

One point for each correct answer.

1. The benmaist bore.
2. Tak the bree wi the barm.
3. Bottomless breeks.
4. Stink like a brock.
5. Tak a fair bucket.
6. Lowsin time.

ROUND SEVEN — Singing and Reciting Games

What actions are the players performing in each of the following?

One point for each correct answer.

1. Nievie-nievie-nick-nack,
   What haun will ye tak?
   Tak the richt or tak the wrang,
   I'll beguile ye if I can.
2. One-two-three-a-leerie,
   Four-five-six-a-leerie,
   Seven-eight-nine-a-leerie,
   Ten-a-leerie-postman.
3. Plainy, clappy, backy, head-and-shoulders etc.
4. Kneel down upon the ground, upon the ground,
        upon the ground,

Kneel down upon the ground, and kiss a bonnie
wee lassie.
5. Stottie ba', stottie ba', tell to me,
How monie bairns am I to hae?
Yin to leeve, and yin to dee,
And yin to sit on its nurse's knee.
6. Wha's afraid o' Black Peter?

ROUND EIGHT — True or False

Say whether the following statements are true or false.

One point for each correct answer. An extra point for
an explanation.

1. A trummlin tam is the appellation given to a man
who, under the influence like Tam O' Shanter,
starts seeing not a dance of witches, but pink
elephants or other such creatures, and starts
shaking uncontrollably.
2. A rockin was a gathering of women to spin and
gossip or, simply, a merrymaking.
3. Nappy is the Scotified version of napkin, and
means a small handkerchief.
4. A backin-turf and a getherin coal performed
much the same function.
5. Tinker's tea was the tea with other, more potent
refreshment, provided at the annual meeting of
the tinkers of a certain clan to crown, or re-elect,
their "king" tinker.
6. A sleepie-mannie was the term applied to a
"stook" of corn blown over by the wind and
lying flat on the ground as if it were asleep.

PROGRAMME FOUR

ROUND ONE — Scots into English Quickies

Note: Three sets of twelve words each are given, these sets being arranged in order of difficulty. For a syndicate quiz, the chairman should choose A, B, or C according to his estimate of the company's knowledge of Scots words. In the case of a panel, it is suggested that each panellist might be asked to choose his/her set in advance, with one point only being awarded for correct answers in set A, two points in set B, and three points in set C.

Pronunciation is given where necessary in brackets.

Give the meanings of the following nouns or naming words:-

Set A	Set B	Set C
1. bizzum	1. cuif/coof	1. chapper-up
2. clowt	2. dowp	2. humplock
3. semmit	3. pawmie	3. bouat *(boo-at)*
4. bubblyjock	4. kebbuck	4. quey *(kwye)*
5. shears	5. laverock	5. blackfuit *(-fit)*
6. doo	6. causey	6. preencod
7. speug	7. clooty dumplin	7. jawbox
8. siller	8. leerie	8. aidle-dub
9. tattie-bogle	9. nickietams	9. collieshangie *("ng" as in "sing")*
10. gallowses	10. claivers *(klayvers)*	10. sneck
11. sark	11. norie	11. quine
12. nieve	12. skelf	12. stirk

ROUND TWO — True or False

Say whether the following statements are true or false.

One point for each correct answer. An extra point for
an explanation.

1. A fitpad means a highwayman who holds up his
    victims on foot.
2. A drucken fuggie-toddler is a Scots expression for
    a man wending his way home, his senses in a
    drunken stupor.
3. The harvest maiden was the last sheaf of corn cut
    at harvest and dressed up as a maiden.
4. A droukit oxter means a thorough wetting in
    which even the armpits are "droukit" or soaked
    with rain.
5. Handfasting was a sort of trial marriage to ensure
    compatibility.
6. A benshee was a sharp-tempered woman who was
    constantly attacking her husband physically
    because of his supposed shortcomings.

ROUND THREE — How did Burns put it?

The following are prose translations, each of two lines
of a Burns poem.

One point given for each line correctly quoted, and
one point for the name of the poem from which the
lines are taken. Three points in all.

1. But allow me to whisper to you the possibility that your looks give no reason for anyone to be tempted by you.
2. Yet you are a lot luckier than I am, since all your concern is simply for the present.
3. It's not possessing great wealth that buys peace and rest.
4. Who will draw the sword of freedom on behalf of the king and the law of the country?
5. And we'll drink a hearty draught of liquor in memory of long ago.
6. Where are you resting in blessed peace now, Mary, dear ghost of the past?

ROUND FOUR — Proverbs.

Supply the missing words with the aid of clues for two points, and give the meaning of the proverb for one point. Each dash stands for a letter.

1. They're fremmit fr - - - - s that canna be fa - - ed (bothered).
2. Hunger's g - - d k - - - - - n.
3. Ilka cock craws cro - - - st on his ain m - - - - n (dungheap).
4. May the mouse ne'er lea your meal-poke wi a - - - - in its - -.
5. Ye canna expect o - - t o' a s - - but a grunt.
6. A bl - - - (timid) cat maks a proud m - - - - -.

ROUND FIVE — Riddles

1. Supply the missing word for a point, and answer
the riddle for a second point.
   Come a riddle, come a riddle, come a rot-tot-tot,
   A wee, wee man in a rid, rid coat,
   A staff in his haun and a - - - - - in his throat,
   Come a riddle, come a riddle, come a rot-tot-tot.

2. Answer the riddle for a point, and give reasons for
the answer for a second point.
   The merle and the blackbird,
   The laverock and the lark;
   The goldie and the gowdspink —
   How monie birds is that?

3. Answer the riddle for a point, and give reasons for
the answer for a second point.
   The laverock and the lark,
   The baukie and the bat,
   The heather-bleat, the mire-snipe (same bird)
   How monie birds is that?

4. Answer the riddle for a point, and give reasons for
the answer for a second point.
   This is the tree that never grew;
   This is the bird that never flew;
   This is the bell that never rang,
   And this the fish that never swam.

5. Who or what is the speaker? What is "oo"? One
point for each correct answer.
   I've made a vow, and I'll keep it true;
   That I'll never stang man through guid sheeps' oo.

6. How much is this in pre-metrical coinage? What is the Scots word for a halfpenny? One point for each correct answer.

A ha'penny here and a ha'penny there,
Fower-pence-ha'penny and a ha'penny mair;
A ha'penny wat and a ha'penny dry,
Fower-pence-ha'penny and a ha'penny forby.

ROUND SIX — How it's said in Scots

What do these expressions mean?

One point for each correct answer.

1. A cat's lick.
2. A causey saint and a house deil.
3. A clockin hen.
4. A johnnie raw.
5. Haud in wi.
6. Tak yin's haun aff.

ROUND SEVEN — What are they in Scots?

Give the Scots for the following objects.

One point for each correct answer.

1.

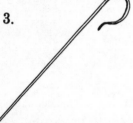

Wooden milk pail with stave projecting for use as handle

2.

A tin drinking mug

3.

Staff with crook

4.

Hard, flat, brightly-coloured sweet often heart-shaped, bearing a sentimental message — much used at children's parties.

5.

Short-stemmed clay smoking pipe

6.

Potato masher

ROUND EIGHT — Mixter-Maxter

How would you make the following?

Up to three points given at the chairman's discretion
for each correct answer.

1. A "peerie" from a "pirn".
2. A windy craw.
3. A snory bane (or button).
4. A hanky parachute.
5. A sooker.
6. A turnip lantern.

PROGRAMME FIVE

ROUND ONE — Scots into English Quickies

Note: Three sets of twelve words each are given, these sets being arranged in order of difficulty. For a syndicate quiz, the chairman should choose A, B, or C according to his estimate of the company's knowledge of Scots words. In the case of a panel, it is suggested that each panellist might be asked to choose his/her set in advance, with one point only being awarded for correct answers in set A, two points in set B, and three points in set C.

Pronunciation is given where necessary in brackets.

Give the meanings of the following adjectives or descriptive words:-

Set A	Set B	Set C
1. claggy	1. bien *(been)*	1. clatchy
2. snell	2. drumly	2. sib
3. boss	3. fushionless	3. braisant
4. leal	4. caller	4. tosh
5. carnaptious	5. mealy-mou'd *(-moo-d)*	5. vieve *(veeve)*
6. dour *(d-oo-r)*	6. fykie	6. trystit
7. drouthy *(dr-oo-thy)*	7. kenspeckle	7. brent
8. glaurie	8. gleg	8. clinty
9. donnert	9. forfochen	9. bunemaist *(binmaist)*
10. near-the-bit	10. camsteerie	10. bausy
11. gallus	11. bowlie *(as in "owl")*	11. chawsome
12. thrawn	12. brosie *(broazie)*	12. broukit *(brookit)*

ROUND TWO — Mixter-Maxter

One point for each correct answer.

1. Which town does a "Bairn" come from?
2. Which town does a "Dounhamer" *(doonhame-er)* come from?
3. Which town does a "Loun" *(loon)* come from?
4. Which town does a "Rid Lichty" come from?
5. St Johnstoun is the old name for which town?
6. Whom do you need a "lang spune" to sup with?

ROUND THREE — Burns Round

Supply the missing line for one point, and give the name of the poem from which it is taken for another point. Each dash stands for a word.

1. — — —, — — —,
   Lovely we thing, wert thou mine . . .
2. — — —, — — — —,
   But juist a drappie in our ee . . .
3. — — — —, — — —,
   And I sae weary, fou *(foo)* o care.
4. — — — — — — —,
   And danced awa wi the exciseman.
5. — — — — — —,
   Need a body cry?
6. — — — — — — —,
   The man's the gowd for aa that.

ROUND FOUR — Proverbs

Supply the missing words with the aid of clues for two points, and give the meaning of the proverb for one point. Each dash stands for a letter.

1. There belangs mair to a b - d nor f - - - - bare legs.
2. A reiky *(reeky)* house and a gi - - - - (complaining) wife
    Will lead a man a fa - - - - - (troublesome) life.
3. Ye canna pit an auld h - - - on young sh - - - - - - s.
4. Speir nae q - - - - - - - - and ye'll be tellt nae - - - -.
5. Ne'er cast a - - - - - till - - - be out.
6. Wha peys the - - - - - ca's the - - - -.

ROUND FIVE — Christian Names

Give the English equivalents of the following.

One point for each correct answer.

1. Leezie
2. Mailie
3. Teenie
4. Phemie/Phame
5. Sime/Symie
6. Tib/Tibbie

ROUND SIX — How it's said in Scots

What do these expressions mean?

One point for each correct answer.

1. High i' the bend.
2. Hover a blink.
3. Come up yin's humph.
4. Nae faurer gaen *(gane)* than.
5. A fiddler's biddin.
6. Gang agley.

ROUND SEVEN — What are they in Scots?

Give the Scots for the following objects.

One point for each correct answer.

1.

cream jug

2.

mallet

3.

china dog

4.

porridge stirrer

5.

top hat

6.

shallow two-handled
drinking cup of wood
or silver

ROUND EIGHT — Farm Words

What are the following?

One point for each correct answer.

1. A bothy.
2. A mairch dyke.
3. A feein fair.
4. Neips.
5. The mains ferm.
6. A stirk.

PROGRAMME SIX

ROUND ONE — Scots into English Quickies

Note: Three sets of twelve words each are given, these sets being arranged in order of difficulty. For a syndicate quiz, the chairman should choose A, B, or C according to his estimate of the company's knowledge of Scots words. In the case of a panel, it is suggested that each panellist might be asked to choose his/her set in advance, with one point only being awarded for correct answers in set A, two points in set B, and three points in set C.

Pronunciation is given where necessary in brackets.

Give the meaning of the following verbs or doing words:-

Set A	Set B	Set C
1. gallivant	1. champ	1. clour (cloor)
2. birl	2. shauchle	2. link
3. kittle	3. maun	3. lout (loot)
4. bowf	4. smirr	4. mane
5. byde	5. syne	5. tyne
6. rax	6. boke	6. breird (breerd)
7. rowe (as in "now")	7. busk	7. begowk
8. smit	8. jalouse	8. lig
9. traik	9. let on	9. cangle ("ng" as in "sing")
10. lowp	10. breinge (breenj)	10. tyauve/ chauve
11. chap	11. glunch	11. thraw
12. slaiger	12. beil (beel)	12. channer

ROUND TWO — Burns Round

The following lines from "Tam o' Shanter" have been
deliberately misquoted. The wrong words are in
italics. Give the correct version for three points.

1. Fast by a *fireside*, *glowing* finely,
    Wi reamin *gless* that drank divinely . . .
2. As *birds* flee hame wi lades o' *wealth*,
    The minutes *sped* their way wi pleasure . . .
3. But pleasures are like *roses* spread,
    You *pluck* the flower, its *beauty* is shed . . .
4. Tam *hurried* on through *mud* and mire,
    Ignoring wind, and rain, and fire . . .
5. Wi *fowerpenny* we fear nae evil;
    Wi *whisky* (Gaelic word) we'll *fecht* the devil . . .
6. Ah Tam! ah Tam! thou'lt *hae* thy *deserts;*
    In hell they'll *fry* ye like a herrin . . .

ROUND THREE — Sentences for Translation

Translate the following sentences into English,
showing you know the meanings of the words
underlined, for three points.

1. Ye'll no be <u>boss</u> by ye get thae parritch ower your
    thrapple.
2. The <u>kail's</u> <u>forrit</u>, sae <u>draw tae</u> and tak your full
    (fuhl).
3. The doun*(doon)*-at-heel auld <u>bauchle</u> <u>trauchlt</u>
    alang the road, her hair aa <u>slaistert</u> wi rain.

4. The wee <u>broukit</u> *(brookit)* bairn <u>dichtit</u> her <u>neb</u> wi her jaiket sleeve.
5. We've been <u>taiglt</u> wi the caur breakin doun *(doon)*, and it'll hae to be <u>Tamson's meir</u> for us the <u>morn's mornin</u> again.
6. <u>The tae hauf</u> are <u>cuifs</u>/coofs, if no <u>evendoun</u> fuils *(fills)*.

ROUND FOUR — Parts of the Body

What are the following?

One point for each correct answer.

1. wame
2. pinkie
3. hurdies
4. haffets
5. hurkle bane
6. hoch

ROUND FIVE — Ailments

One point for each correct answer.

What would be wrong with you if you were —
1. gam-teetht?
2. hippit?

3. bou-hocht?
4. forfochen?

What would be wrong with you if you had —

5. the scoot?
6. a curmurrin in the guts?

ROUND SIX — How it's said in Scots

What do these expressions mean?

One point for each correct answer.

1. Gee *(jee)* yin's ginger.
2. Creish *(kreesh)* the luif*(lif)*/loof.
3. Doun *(doon)* i' the mou *(moo)*.
4. A dreipin *(dreepin)* roast.
5. Nae smaa drink.
6. A drappie in the ee.

ROUND SEVEN — Mixter-Maxter

What do the following "pennies" mean?

One point for each correct answer.

1. penny jo.
2. penny buff.
3. penny fee.
4. penny geggie.
5. penny wheep.
6. penny waddin.

ROUND EIGHT — Proverbs

Supply the missing words with the aid of clues for two points, and give the meaning of the proverb for one point. Each dash stands for a letter.

1. Gie your p - - - - to your wife and ye may as weel gie her your br - - - s into the bargain.
2. As the day - - - - - - - - - -, the cauld - - - - - - - - - - - -.
3. He that w - - l to Cupar, ma - - n to Cupar.
4. A bonny br - - - is sune *(sin)* b - - - it.
5. An ill c - o may hae a guid c - - f.
6. A new b - - - - m s - - ps clean.

PROGRAMME SEVEN

ROUND ONE — Scots into English Quickies

Note: Three sets of twelve words each are given, these sets being arranged in order of difficulty. For a syndicate quiz, the chairman should choose A, B, or C according to his estimate of the company's knowledge of Scots words. In the case of a panel, it is suggested that each panellist might be asked to choose his/her set in advance, with one point only being awarded for correct answers in set A, two points in set B, and three points in set C.

Pronunciation is given where necessary in brackets.

Give the meanings of the following nouns or naming words:-

Set A	Set B	Set C
1. pow	1. cockie-leekie	1. rickle
2. braws	2. mercat	2. snood
3. haivers	3. clug	3. cleuch
		(clooch — guttural)
4. jennie-meggie	4. clashbag	4. merse
5. gumption	5. blecknin	5. clamjamfry
6. clype	6. crichle	6. leister
7. blue dykie	7. chitterin-bite	7. bucht
8. mennen	8. tattie-ploum	8. brace
9. worset	9. swatch	9. winnock
10. whang	10. coom	10. cowt
11. stour	11. curfuffle	11. creepie-stool
12. cushie doo	12. yella yite	12. thairm
(cooshie)		

ROUND TWO — Proverbs

Supply the missing words with the aid of clues, for
two points, and give the meaning of the proverb for
one point. Each dash stands for a letter.

1. An a - - (meaning early) winter's a s - - r winter.
   (Words rhyme)
2. Ill wan g - - r is aye ill wa - - d (meaning spent).
3. A fou *(foo)* wa - - maks a stra - - - t back.
4. Bel - ve (meaning soon) is twa o - - s and a half.
5. A g - - k (meaning fool) 'll no be bricht at
   Be - tane (1st day of May).
6. He that winna l - - t (meaning bend) and lift a
   pr - - n will ne'er be worth a groat.

ROUND THREE — Sentences for Translation

Translate the following sentences into English,
showing you know the meaning of the words and
phrases underlined, for three points.

1. See me my bannet and I'll toddle up by and see
   how the beasts are tholin the wather.
2. Tak tent, my man. The jaud 'll hae her wull o ye
   yet.
3. Ye'll be for an early rise the morn, seein ye're
   ettlin to tak the gate by seiven o'clock.
4. Ye sleekit we nyaff! Ye're braw and able to dae
   the job your lane.
5. Ye're lookin geylies doun i' the mou *(moo)* the
   day, laddie. Wha's stolen your scone?

6. There's a <u>gorlin</u> <u>flauchterin</u> about the front <u>green.</u>

ROUND FOUR — What are they in Scots?

Give the Scots for the following objects.

One point for each correct answer.

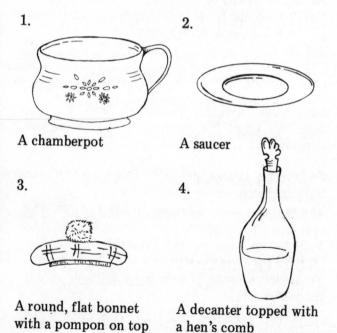

1.

A chamberpot

2.

A saucer

3.

A round, flat bonnet
with a pompon on top

4.

A decanter topped with
a hen's comb

5.

6.

A small stool with a hole
in the middle of seat for
lifting with finger

A sickle or reaping hook

ROUND FIVE — Burns Round

Give the meanings of the words in italics in these lines
from various Burns poems, for three points.

1. ... Till a' their weel-swalled *kytes* belyve
    Are bent like drums.
    Then auld guid man, maist like to *rive*,
    Bethankit hums.

                              "To a Haggis"

2. Clap in his *walie nieve* a blade,
    He'll mak it whissle;
    And legs, and arms, and heid will *sned*
    Like taps o thrissle.

                              "To a Haggis"

3. He was a *gash* and faithful *tyke*
    As ever lap a sheuch or dyke.
    His honest, sonsie, *bawsent* face
    Aye gat him friends in ilka place.

                              "The Twa Dogs"

4.   But gin ye be a brig as auld as me,
     Though faith, that date I doubt ye'll never see;
     There'll be, if that day come, I'll *wad* a *bodle*,
     Some fewer *whigmaleeries* in your noddle.
                                    "The Twa Brigs"
5.   A guid New Year I wish thee, Maggie!
     Hae, there's a *ripp* to thy auld baggie;
     Though thou's *howe-backit*, now, and *knaggie*,
     I've see the day . . .
                            "The Auld Farmer's Salutation"
6.   Auld *baudrons* by the ingle sits,
     And wi her loof her face a-washin;
     But Willie's wife is nae sae trig,
     She *dichts* her grunzie wi a *hushion*.
                                    "Sic a Wife as Willie had"

ROUND SIX — How it's said in Scots

What do these expressions mean?

One point for each correct answer.

1.   To go halfers.
2.   To mak naethin o't.
3.   To birl the wulkies.
4.   To rin the gless.
5.   To claw somebody's back.
6.   To caw the crack.

ROUND SEVEN — Christian Names

Give the English equivalents of the following.

One point for each correct answer.

1. Sibbie
2. Ailie
3. Mamie
4. Minnie
5. Nan
6. Eck

ROUND EIGHT — Teasers

What are the following?

One point for each correct answer.

1. A cuttin loaf
2. Bottomless breeks
3. A curly-heidit chisel
4. A drap o the auld kirk
5. A Scotch canary
6. A sammy dreip

ANSWERS — PROGRAMME ONE

ROUND ONE — Scots into English Quickies

Set A	Set B	Set C
1. halfpenny piece	1. conduit; sewer	1. hoarfrost
2. direction	2. hook; sickle	2. steps on house gable
3. worn-out shoe; old, feeble person	3. harvest	3. brains
4. cloth	4. owl	4. wood roof lining
5. trousers	5. manure fork	5. horse collar
6. jug	6. fire	6. throat
7. soup	7. drinking cup	7. close-fitting tartan trousers
8. ditch; gutter	8. rowan tree	8. pivot used to suspend pots over fire
9. pinafore	9. scavenger	9. gimlet
10. chest	10. cow dung	10. teapot
11. teacher's strap	11. pool, pond	11. two-roomed cottage
12. flame	12. mole	12. spigot

ROUND TWO — Mixter-Maxter

1. You would be accompanying a friend back to his home, or half-way back, or to his home and part of the way back again, according to which part of the country you lived in.
2. I never saw the equal of that porridge before.
3. He would be sulking.
4. He would mean broth warmed up a second time — or, a story or sermon given over and over again.
5. He would be scolding you.
6. He would be intending to put on dry shoes and stockings.

ROUND THREE — True or False

1. False. A teuch jean was a jujube, or sugar-and-gum lozenge.

2. False. "Caw" here means to drive, not to call.
3. True. The bink(ie) was the (small) bench on which he sat and whistled.
4. False. "Caller oo!" means "Fresh oysters!" and was the cry of fishwives selling oysters in the nineteenth century for a penny for twelve.
5. True. It was another name for a swallow-tail coat.
6. False. "Pig" is the Scots word for potsherd or broken piece of earthenware. The expression was adopted into English from the Scots.

ROUND FOUR — How did Burns put it?

1. When chapman billes leave the street,
   And drouthy neibours neibours meet . . .
                   From "Tam o' Shanter"
2. They gang in stirks and come out asses,
   Plain truth to speak . . .
                   From "Epistle to John Lapraik"
3. But yet, O Lord, confess I must,
   At times I'm fashed we fleshly lust . . .
                   From "Holy Willie's Prayer"
4. When lyart leaves bestrew the yird,
   Or wavering like the baukie bird . . .
                   From "The Jolly Beggars"
5. Auld Scotland wants nae skinking ware
   That jaups in luggies . . .
                   From "To a Haggis"
6. O wad some Power the giftie gie us,
   To see oursels as others see us!
                   From "To a Louse"

ROUND FIVE — Christian Names

1. Andrew
2. Margaret
3. George
4. Euphemia

5. Gilbert
6. Christina

ROUND SIX — How it's said in Scots

1. The old routine
2. Upset someone's barrow — i.e. upset someone's plans.
3. The manager
4. Take a thing badly
5. It will serve him right
6. Not an article of clothing to wear

ROUND SEVEN — What are they in Scots?

1. girr
2. truan/trewan
3. claut
4. tawse
5. ladle
6. baffs

ROUND EIGHT — Quote Round

(Note that names of poets where known are supplied simply as extra information)

1. Chairlie's; main; hert.
   "Will ye no come back again?" (by Lady Nairne)
2. wearin; wreaths; leal.
   "The Land o the Leal" (by Lady Nairne)
3. weep; youngest; son.
   "Jock o Hazeldean" (by Sir Walter Scott)
4. bane; blue; theik/theek.
   "The Twa Corbies" (Ballad — anonymous)
5. weit/weet; played; aboon/abune.
   "Sir Patrick Spens" (Ballad — anonymous)
6. wae; loaning; flowers.
   "The Flowers of the Forest" (by Jean Elliot)

Answers — Programme Two

ROUND ONE — Scots into English Quickies

Set A	Set B	Set C
1. empty	1. alert; lively	1. contented; comfortable; cordial
2. left-handed	2. fastidious	2. dejected
3. weakly	3. dull; stupid	3. frightful; unearthly
4. sly; hypocritical	4. slippery	4. foreign; strange
5. reluctant	5. prim; affected in speech	5. half dried off
6. shrivelled	6. shrunken; emaciated	6. curious
7. low	7. skilful	7. extraordinary
8. bashful; timid	8. slender	8. sensitive; tender
9. brittle	9. fastidious	9. certain
10. cautious	10. sedate; decorous	10. sly; deft
11. dirty; messy	11. incompetent; worthless	11. old-fashioned; wise beyond one's years
12. high	12. flabby; spongy	12. stained with tears.

ROUND TWO — Proverbs

1. **water; stirkie.** There is always a very good cause for an unfortunate happening.
2. **gear; bouk** *(book)*. A capable person is often also a small one in stature.
3. **bairns; beetle.** He who gives away all his possessions to his children should have the brains pounded out of him.
4. **bum; banes.** A good spanking never did any harm.
5. **coo; tail.** Fail in one small detail after being so near to success.
6. **bannets; waitin.** Don't be so choosy as to miss your chance completely.

ROUND THREE — Burns Round

1. But hand in hand we'll go . . .
   "John Anderson, my Jo"
2. A clapper tongue wad deave a miller . . .
   "Sic a Wife as Willie had"/"Willie Wastle'·
3. And the rocks melt wi the sun . . .
   "A red, red Rose"
4. Return sae dowf and weary, O.
   "My ain kind Dearie, O"
5. The dance gaed through the lighted haa . . .
   "Mary Morison"
6. My bonnie dearie.
   "Caw the Yowes"

ROUND FOUR — Food

1. Boiled potatoes dipped in some sort of relish.
2. Roasted apples.
3. Oat husks steeped, fermented, and boiled into a pudding.
4. Porridge of boiling water or milk mixed with oatmeal, salt, and butter added.
5. Potatoes stewed with onions.
6. Oatmeal and onion fry.

ROUND FIVE — True or False

1. False. It is a humming beetle.
2. True. They are blown by children to tell the time by the number of puffs taken to clear all the fluff off.
3. False. It is a "drink at the door", or a stirrup cup.
4. False. It is the cry set up on April Fools' Day when someone is caught out with a plausible story.
5. True. You knock or "chap" on the table to indicate that you can't play.
6. True. Adulterers and wife beaters were mounted on a "stang" or pole, and carried and beaten through the streets by the onlookers.

ROUND SIX — How it's said in Scots

1. Take a drink.
2. Pedal a cycle.
3. The middle of the roadway.
4. Defy.
5. A person who is always complaining.
6. Clotted or curdled milk.

ROUND SEVEN — Sentences for Translation

1. Consult a looking-glass too often and you'll see a fool behind it. (Yourself!)
2. I visited the old miser while he was at his tea, and he never as much as invited me to have something to eat.
3. You'll never find a ringed worm (for fishing) in a dunghill of fresh manure.
4. The boy will have done with his mischievous behaviour before he is much older.
5. That stupid, contemptible little fellow will never do anything worth while.
6. She was a peevish, stubborn, ill-natured old hussy.

ROUND EIGHT — Mixter-Maxter

1. The player who was "het" turned away and counted "Five-ten-double-ten-five-ten-a-hundred", while the other players sneaked up on him from behind. When the former had finished counting he turned swiftly, and if he caught another player moving instead of standing like a "stookie", that other player was either counted out, or became "het" in turn.
2. One boy was chosen to kick the can along the street as far as he could. Another boy who was "het" ran after it and brought it back to the den or base while the other players hid. The one who was "het" then looked for the hidden players and brought them back to the den, but if one player ran out from hiding and kicked the can away again, the prisoners were freed and the whole process had to be

repeated.

3. A button was placed in the centre of a circle, and each player threw in another button in turn. The player whose button landed nearest to the target button was allowed to pick up both it and as many other buttons as he could by pressing the thumb into the button hollow. During the "season", mothers were driven frantic sewing buttons onto buttonless trousers!

4. Two boys stood each on his own goal-line, taking turns at trying to head the ball over his opponent's line.

5. Four pebbles were spread on a square, or a flat stone, while another pebble was cast into the air. The four "square" pebbles had to be picked up and the thrown pebble caught in the same hand before it reached the ground.

6. The player threw a round, flat piece of marble or other stone, or a tin lid, into a "bed" of chalked squares, each square in turn, then kicked it on by hopping on one foot, trying to avoid having either the peever or the foot land on any of the chalked lines.

ANSWERS — PROGRAMME THREE

ROUND ONE — Scots into English Quickies

Set A	Set B	Set C
1. wipe	1. whistle	1. build
2. dip; bathe	2. roast; broil	2. write
3. drench	3. potter; splash about	3. bless
4. grope with hand; muddle	4. clean up; get in order	4. celebrate with a gift
5. duck; elude	5. delay; detain	5. endure
6. ask	6. take notice of; care for	6. sneer; titter
7. loosen	7. thatch	7. eat dirtily; swallow noisily
8. shiver	8. assert dogmatically	8. tingle; throb
9. bend; cower	9. wrinkle; crease	9. select
10. dispute	10. wane, decline in health	10. fret; complain
11. weep	11. cause; compel	11. itch
12. grunt	12. overturn	12. flutter

ROUND TWO — Proverbs

1. **tocherless; hame.** A penniless/dowerless woman will wait a long while before she gets married.
2. **ettle; whyles.** Try often and you will occasionally succeed.
3. **cog; kail.** Seize every chance that presents itself.
4. **wyce; breeks.** It is a wise wife who leaves her husband in control.
5. **laich; lang.** Don't be over-ambitious if you want to stay the pace.
6. **fuil/fool; siller.** A fool can never keep hold of his money.

ROUND THREE — Burns Round

1. swats for beer; noddle for heid; boddle for faurthen.
2. grannie for mammy; sark for shirt; coft for bocht.
3. glowered for watched; amazed for bumbazed; furious for riotous.
4. fidged for wriggled; fain for eagerly; blew for puffed.
5. weel for often; skellum for rogue; bletherin for talkative.
6. dames for wives; gars for makes; monie for often.

ROUND FOUR — Sentences for Translation

1. It's not good for a stunted little person like her to be roaming all over the town in such weather.
2. You senseless big fool! You should be very deeply ashamed of yourself!
3. A sickly child was said long ago to have been subjected to a glance from the evil eye.
4. If you were wise, you would be getting on your way home before the public houses closed.
5. Trundle your hoop with your own hooked rod.
6. I see the farmer who occupies Oldhill is well on with his ploughing this year.

ROUND FIVE — Christian Names

1. Albert
2. Robina
3. Griselda
4. Laurence
5. Elizabeth
6. Marian

ROUND SIX — How it's said in Scots

1. The innermost recess.
2. Take the rough with the smooth.
3. The kilt.
4. Smell like a badger.
5. Be a hard drinker.
6. Time for finishing work for the day.

ROUND SEVEN — Singing and Reciting Games

1. This is the rhyme spoken in a guessing game, in which the reciter clenches his hands and invites his opponent to guess in which of the hands an article is hidden.
2. The player, a girl, is bouncing a ball, passing it once beneath her uplifted leg at each "a-leerie", and twice at "ten-a-leerie-postman".
3. The player, a girl, is throwing a ball against a wall, and performing the "clappy" etc. actions before catching the ball on the rebound.
4. These are two of the lines sung in the game, bee-baw-babbity, in which boys and girls join hands and dance round a player in the centre. This player kneels at the words, "Kneel down , , ," in front of one of the opposite sex in the ring, and they kiss and change places, and the game goes on as before.
5. The girl is bouncing a ball on the ground while reciting these lines to the rhythm of the ball bouncing.
6. This is called out by a child at some distance from the rest of the players and with his back to them. "No me!" they cry, and come gradually nearer till the boy finally turns and chases them.

ROUND EIGHT — True or False

1. False. It is the name given to either potted meat or a table jelly.

2. True. It got its name from the "rock" or distaff used in spinning.
3. False. It means ale or beer.
4. True. They were put on a fire last thing at night to damp it down and keep it burning till morning.
5. False. It was tea brewed in a pan over a fire instead of in a teapot. (A tinker was of course a dealer in pots and pans — tin-ker).
6. False. It is a mote in the eye.

ANSWERS — PROGRAMME FOUR

ROUND ONE — Scots into English Quickies

Set A	Set B	Set C
1. broomstick; loose, worthless woman	1. fool	1. one who knocked on doors to wake up factory workers
2. blow; slap	2. buttocks; cigarette end	2. hillock
3. vest; undershirt	3. stroke with strap	3. hand lantern
4. turkey	4. a cheese	4. heifer
5. scissors	5. lark	5. lovers' intermediary
6. dove	6. cobbled street	6. pin cushion
7. sparrow	7. dumpling wrapped in muslin cloth	7. kitchen sink
8. silver; money	8. lamplighter	8. cesspool
9. scarecrow	9. straps or strings round trouser legs to keep out dust etc.	9. brawl; dogfight
10. man's braces	10. chatter	10. bolt; latch
11. shirt	11. whim	11. girl; hussy
12. fist	12. splinter	12. bullock.

ROUND TWO — True or False

1. False. It means a footpath.
2. False. It is a small yellow bee that "toddles" or crawls over the "fog" or moss as if it were drunk.
3. True. It was then given to the farmer's wife, who hung it on the wall over the fireplace till the following spring, when it was given to the horses that ploughed the first new furrow.
4. False. It means a good dowry (a guid tocher).

5. True. Couples often cohabited for this purpose, and if the relationship wasn't to the liking of either after a year and a day, they could separate without any stigma being attached to the woman. Any child born was put in the father's care.
6. False. It was a supernatural being who wailed outside a house to announce the approaching death of a member of the family.

ROUND THREE — How did Burns put it?

1. But let me whisper in your lug,
   Ye're aiblins nae temptation.
   > From "Address to the Unco Guid"
2. Still thou are blest, compared wi me!
   The present only toucheth thee . . .
   > From "To a Mouse"
3. It's no in wealth like Lon'on bank
   To purchase peace and rest.
   > From "Epistle to Davie"
4. Wha for Scotand's king and law,
   Freedom's sword will strongly draw . . .?
   > From "Scot wha Hae" or "Bruce's
   > Address to His Army at Bannockburn"
5. And we'll tak a richt guidwillie waucht,
   For auld lang syne.
   > From "Auld Lang Syne"
6. O Mary, dear departed shade,
   Where is thy place of blissful rest . . .?
   > From "To Mary in Heaven"

ROUND FOUR — Proverb

1. friends; fashed. They are strange friends who can't be bothered to give you a helping hand.
2. guid; kitchen. A hungry person doesn't need any relish to add to the taste of the food.
3. crousest *(croosest)*; midden. Persons act more confidently

in familiar surroundings.

4. tear; ee. May you always have plenty of food in your larder.
5. ocht; sou *(soo)*. A base person will always act basely.
6. blate; mouse. A timid warden is taken advantage of by those in his charge.

ROUND FIVE — Riddles

1. Stane. The answer is a cherry.
2. Three. There are two names for the same bird in each line.
3. Two. The bat isn't a bird.
4. The arms of Glasgow. They consist of a tree, a bird, a bell, and a fish.
5. An adder; oo means wool.
6. A shilling; bawbee.

ROUND SIX — How it's said in Scots

1. A hasty wash.
2. A person who is genial abroad and bad-tempered at home.
3. A brood hen.
4. A country lout.
5. Curry favour with.
6. Strike with one's hand.

ROUND SEVEN — What are they in Scots?

1. a hannie/haunie, or it could also be a cog/coggie, depending on size
2. tinnie
3. crummock
4. readin sweetie
5. cutty/cutty-cley *(clye)*
6. tattie-beetle

ROUND EIGHT — Mixter-Maxter

1. To make a peerie or spinning top, cut the end off a wooden thread bobbin, then push a pointed wooden pin through the bobbin hole and twirl the top end of the pin with thumb and finger to set the peerie going.

2. Stick a fairly large potato full of seagull or crow feathers, and set it on the ground so it will be propelled along by the wind in the sail-like feathers.

3. Attach a string to a pig's leg bone so as to form a loop on either side of the bone — or simply pass the ends of a piece of fine thread through two opposite holes in a large button and tie them to form a loop on either side of button. These loops are then passed over the backs of the hands and after a few "birls" are alternately slackened and pulled tight to set the bone or button whirling round.

4. Tie strings of equal length to the four corners of a handkerchief, then attach the other ends of the strings to a fairly heavy stone. The whole is then thrown into the air, to open and descent gracefully to the ground.

5. Attach a strong piece of string to a round piece of leather about three inches in diameter, through a hole in the middle of the leather. The leather is then soaked and pressed hard down on any flat-surfaced article you wish to raise by suction.

6. Slice a large turnip across the shoulder and pare out the inside till it is quite hollow. Cut a face on the outside skin, attach a string to opposite sides as a handle, set a candle inside and light it, and replace the sliced-off lid.

ANSWERS — PROGRAMME FIVE

ROUND ONE — Scots into English Quickies

Set A	Set B	Set C
1. sticky	1. affluent; cosy	1. muddy
2. cold; sharp	2. muddy	2. related
3. empty	3. dull; tasteless	3. bold; insolent
4. loyal	4. cool; fresh	4. tidy; pleasant
5. bad-tempered	5. plausible	5. lively; vivid
6. obstinate	6. fussy; exacting	6. bespoken, invited
7. thirsty	7. prominent; remarkable	7. smooth
8. muddy	8. alert, nimble	8. flinty; stony
9. stupid; stupefied	9. exhausted	9. topmost
10. mean	10. unruly; wild	10. big and fat
11. daring; rash	11. crooked; bent	11. disappointing
12. stubborn; surly	12. course; stout	12. tear-stained

ROUND TWO — Mixter-Maxter

1. Falkirk
2. Dumfries
3. Forfar
4. Arbroath
5. Perth
6. A Fifer

ROUND THREE — Burns Round

1. Bonnie wee thing, canny wee thing . . .
          "Bonnie Wee Thing"
2. We arena fou *(foo)*, we're nae that fou . . .
          "O, Willie brewed a Peck o' Maut"

3. How can ye chant, ye little birds . . .
>"Ye Banks and Braes"

4. The deil cam fiddlin through the toun *(toon)* . . .
>"The Deil's awa wi the Exciseman"

5. Gin a body kiss a body . . .
>"Comin through the Rye"

6. The rank is but the guinea's stamp . . .
>"Is there for honest Poverty" or "A Man's a Man"

ROUND FOUR — Proverbs

1. Bed; fower. There is more to a marriage than lying together in bed.
2. girnin; fashous. A man who lives in a poor sort of house along with a complaining wife has a lifetime of trouble on his hands.
3. heid; shouthers *(shoothers)*. It's impossible to give young people the wisdom of their elders.
4. questions; lees. If you don't ask questions, you won't be told any lies.
5. clout *(cloot)*; mey/may. Don't dispense with any clothing till the hawthorn blossom appears. (The alternative, the end of the month of May, will be accepted).
6. piper; tune. One has the right of choice when one is doing the paying.

ROUND FIVE — Christian Names

1. Elizabeth
2. Molly
3. Christina
4. Euphemia
5. Simon
6. Elizabeth

ROUND SIX — How it's said in Scots

1. Haughty: ambitious.
2. Wait a moment.
3. Come into one's mind.
4. As recently as.
5. A last-minute invitation.
6. Go awry; miscarry.

ROUND SEVEN — What are they in Scots?

1. pourie
2. mell
3. wallie dug
4. spurtle
5. lum hat
6. quaich

ROUND EIGHT — Farm Words

1. Farm servant's quarters.
2. Boundary fence.
3. Fair at which farmers engaged servants.
4. Turnips.
5. Home farm on an estate.
6. Young ox/steer.

ANSWERS — PROGRAMME SIX

ROUND ONE — Scots into English Quickies

Set A	Set B	Set C
1. gad about	1. mash	1. beat; strike
2. rotate	2. shuffle; shamble	2. stride; trip lightly
3. tickle	3. must	3. stoop; curtsy
4. bark	4. drizzle	4. lament
5. stay; endure	5. rinse	5. lose
6. stretch	6. retch; gush forth	6. germinate
7. roll	7. dress; make ready	7. deceive
8. infect	8. conjecture; suspect	8. lie
9. gad about	9. divulge	9. quibble
10. leap	10. push forward impetuously	10. struggle
11. knock; hammer	11. frown	11. twist
12. besmear	12. fester	12. complain

ROUND TWO — Burns Round

1. ingle for fireside; bleizin for glowing; swats for gless.
2. bees for birds; treasure for wealth; winged for sped.
3. poppies for roses; seize for pluck; bloom for beauty.
4. skelpit for hurried; dub for mud; despising for ignoring.
5. tippenny for fowerpenny; usquebae for whisky; face for fecht.
6. get for hae; fairin for deserts; roast for fry.

ROUND THREE — Sentences for Translation

1. Your stomach won't be empty by the time you get that porridge down your throat.
2. The soup has been brought in, so bring your chair up to the

table and eat as much as you wish.
3. The down-at-the-heel old woman trudged along the road, her hair all clapped down with the rain.
4. The little tear-stained/soiled child wiped her nose with her jacket sleeve.
5. We have been delayed with the car breaking down, and we'll have to walk tomorrow morning again.
6. The one half are louts, if not downright fools.

ROUND FOUR — Parts of the Body

1. stomach
2. little finger
3. buttocks
4. temples
5. hip bone
6. lower thigh

ROUND FIVE — Ailments

1. You'd have misshapen/overlapping teeth.
2. You'd be lame with thigh strain.
3. You'd be bandy-legged.
4. You'd be physically exhausted.
5. You'd have diarrhoea.
6. You'd have a rumbling stomach.

ROUND SIX — How it's said in Scots

1. Bother oneself.
2. Bribe; give a gratuity.
3. Downcast.
4. A good source of income.
5. Of no small importance, of a person.
6. Enough drink to make slightly drunk.

ROUND SEVEN — Mixter-Maxter

1. A prostitute.
2. A school primer.
3. Wages.
4. A travelling theatre show.
5. Weak ale.
6. Wedding at which guests paid to get in.

ROUND EIGHT — Proverbs

1. purse; breeks. Let your wife have charge of the money, and she'll take control of all else as well.
2. lengthens; strengthens. The cold weather in winter comes after the turning of the sun.
3. will; maun. You can't stop a stubborn person doing what he wants.
4. bride; buskit. An attractive bride doesn't need much dressing up.
5. coo; cauf. Good may come from an unpromising source.
6. bizzum; soups *(soops)*. Anything new, or anyone new to a task, makes a good job of it. (There is an unstated "but" at the end of it).

ANSWERS — PROGRAMME SEVEN

ROUND ONE — Scots into English Quickies

Set A	Set B	Set C
1. head	1. chicken and leek soup	1. loose pile
2. best clothes	2. market	2. hair ribbon
3. nonsense	3. log of wood; wooden shoe	3. crag; coal pit
4. cranefly	4. gossip	4. flat rich ground by river
5. intelligence	5. boot polish	5. mob; rabble
6. tell-tale	6. wheeziness in throat	6. three-pronged fish spear
7. hedge sparrow	7. food taken after bathing	7. sheep fold
8. minnow	8. the fruit on the potato plant after flowering	8. mantelshelf
9. wool	9. sample	9. window
10. thong	10. soot	10. colt
11. dust	11. disorder; excitement	11. three-legged stool; church stool of repentance
12. wood-pigeon	12. yellow hammer	12. catgut; fiddle string

ROUND TWO — Proverbs

1. air; sair. When winter comes early, it is likely to be a hard one.
2. gear; wared. Wealth that has been badly come by will also be spent badly.
3. wame; straucht. When a man is prosperous, he will bear himself accordingly.
4. belyve; oors. When a person says he will do a thing

presently, you can be sure it won't be done for some considerable time.

5. gowk; Beltane. Once a fool, always a fool.
6. lout. preen. He that won't bother himself over a job that gives little reward will never make much of it.

ROUND THREE — Sentences for Translation

1. Give me my bonnet and I'll saunter up the road and see how the cattle are facing up to the rough weather.
2. Be heedful, my man. The perverse woman will get her own way with you yet.
3. You'll be intending to get up out of bed early tomorrow, since you're aiming to get on your way before seven o'clock.
4. You sly little nobody! You're very well able to do the job by yourself.
5. You're looking rather dejected today, lad. Who's taken advantage of you?
6. There's a small fledgling bird fluttering around on the front lawn.

ROUND FOUR — What are they in Scots?

1. po; chanty; jordan
2. flet
3. tam-o-shanter
4. tappit hen
5. currie
6. heuk

ROUND FIVE — Burns Round

1. kytes means stomachs; rive means burst; bethankit means grace after meal.

2. walie means ample; nieve means fist; sned means lop off.
3. gash means animated or clever; tyke means dog; bawsent means white-streaked.
4. wad means wager; bodle means a small coin; whigmaleeries means whims.
5. ripp means handful of corn; howe-backit means hollow-backed; knaggie means bony.
6. baudrons means cat; dichts means wipes; hushion means a stocking with the foot worn away.

ROUND SIX — How it's said in Scots

1. To divide into half shares.
2. To show no improvement.
3. To turn somersault.
4. To use up the allotted time.
5. To flatter someone.
6. To converse.

ROUND SEVEN — Christian Names

1. Isabel(la)
2. Alison
3. Jemima; Marion
4. Mary; Marion
5. Agnes; Ann
6. Alexander

ROUND EIGHT — Teasers

1. A yesterday's/day-old loaf
2. The kilt
3. A chisel with the handle-end frayed through hammering
4. A dram of whisky
5. A yellow hammer
6. A spiritless person

WHA'LL BEAR THE GREE?

WHA'LL BEAR THE GREE?
(Who'll win the prize?)

Following are sets of questions suitable for putting to the syndicate quiz finalists. (See Introduction)

SET A

1. What is the meaning of the noun, manawdge *(manodj)*? (1)
2. What is the meaning of the verb, to fleich *(fleetch)*? (1)
3. What is the meaning of the proverb, "Early maister, sune *(sin)* knave"? (1)
4. What is the meaning of the proverb, "Keep your gab steikit *(steekit)* whan ye dinna ken your company"? (1)
5. Following is a verse of a certain poem. Give the meanings of the words underlined for three points, and the name of the poem for one point. (4)

> "I' faith," quo Johnnie, "I got a <u>fleg,</u>
> Wi their <u>claymores</u> and <u>philabegs</u>;
> If I face them again, deil brak my legs!
> So I wish you a guid mornin."

6. What is the meaning of the phrase, to speak pan loaf? (1)
7. What is the meaning of the phrase, pease brose and piannaes? (1)
8. Supply the missing line in the following, taken from a Burns poem, for one point, and give the name of the poem for one point: (2)

> Then gently scan your brother man,
> — — — — (four words)

9. Supply the missing line as for question 8. (2)
>> But day and nicht my fancy's flicht
>> — — — — — (five words)

10. Say whether the following statement is true or false, for one point. An extra point will be given for a correct explanation: (2)
>> A blin tam was the name given to soldiers returned, maimed or blind, from the Napoleonic Wars.

SET B

1. What is the meaning of the noun, messan? (1)
2. What is the meaning of the adjective, menseless? (1)
3. What is the meaning of the proverb, "A flichter-lichtie's aye in the mune or the midden"? (1)
4. What is the meaning of the proverb, "It's ower late to jouk when the heid's aff"? (1)
5. Following is a verse of a certain poem. Give the meanings of the words underlined for three points, and the name of the poem for one point. (4)
>> He played a march to battle, it cam
>> <u>dirlin</u> through the mist,
>> Till the <u>halflin</u> squared his shoulders and
>> made up his mind to 'list;
>> He tried a <u>spring</u> for wooers, though he
>> wistna what it meant,
>> But the kitchen lass was lauchin and he
>> thocht she maybe kent.

6. What is the meaning of the phrase, aa ae oo? (1)

7. What is the meaning of the phrase, auld i' the horn? (1)
8. Supply the missing part-line in the following, taken from a Burns poem, for one point, and give the name of the poem for one point: (2)

> November chill blaws loud *(lood)* wi angry souch *(sooch — guttural)*;
> The shortening — — — — — (six words)

9. Supply the missing line etc. as for question 8. (2)

> Maggie coost her heid fou *(foo)* heich *(heech — guttural)*,
> — — — — (five words)

10. Say whether the following statement is true or false, for one point. An extra point will be given for a correct explanation: (2)

> The Flowers o' Edinburgh is the title of a lament for the young men killed at the disastrous battle of Flodden.

SET C

1. What is the meaning of the noun, orraman? (1)
2. What is the meaning of the adjective, steive *(steeve)*? (1)
3. What is the meaning of the proverb, "To be ower auld a hen to be trystit ben the barn wi caff"? (1)
4. What is the meaning of the proverb, "An auld seck is aye skailin"? (1)
5. What is the English for the Scots Christian name, Nansie? (1)
6. How many of these words do you think were borrowed by English from Scots: (1)
gillie; flunkey; caddie; strontian; hostel; palliasse?

7. What is the meaning of the phrase, black affrontit? (1)
8. What is the meaning of the phrase, come the peter ower? (1)
9. Supply the missing words in the following lines from Tam o' Shanter, for three points. Each dash stands for a letter. (3)

> Ae - - - - - - brought off her master - - - -,
> But left behind her ain - - - - tail.

10. Say whether the following statement is true or false, for one point. An extra point will be given for any added relevant comment. (2)

> A back-creel was a large basket fitted round the breast with a broad strap and used for carrying manure out of the farm byre to the midden, and from there out to the fields.

SET D

1. What is the meaning of the noun, sourock (soorock)? (1)
2. What is the meaning of the verb, to collogue (co-log)? (1)
3. What is the meaning of the proverb, "Dinna cast awa the cog when the coo flings"? (1)
4. What is the meaning of the proverb, "Ye canna mak a silk purse out o' a sou's (soo's) lug"? (1)
5. Complete the following: (1)

> Sticks and stanes 'll brek my banes,
> But — — — — — (five words)

6. What is the meaning of the expression, Gie somebody his coffee? (1)

7. What is the meaning of the expression, Dae a
   thing aff-loof? (1)
8. What is the English form of the Scots Christian
   name, Abe? (1)
9. "There's the end o' an auld sang," said the
   Scottish chancellor, the Earl of Seafield. What
   was the end of an auld sang? (1)
10. It is almost impossible to keep sometimes from
    being sour. This is a prose translation of what two
    lines from Burns's poetry? This for one point. An
    extra point will be given for the name of the
    poem. (2)

SET E

1. What is the meaning of the verb, to niffer? (1)
2. What is the meaning of the noun, thairm-scraper?
   (1)
3. What is the meaning of the proverb, "Keep your
   ain fish-guts for your ain sea-maws." (1)
4. What is the meaning of the proverb, "He isna
   worth weel that winna byde wae"? (1)
5. Say whether the following statement is true or
   false, for one point. An extra point will be given
   for any relevant comment. (2)

> The boukin *(bookin)* was the annual
> washing of clothes by steeping.

6. Say whether the following statement is true or
   false, for one point. An extra point will be given
   for any relevant comment. (2)

> A christenin bit was the name given,
> when a child was baptised, to an old

boot which must have a hole in the sole, and was hung above the fireplace for luck.

7. What is the meaning of the expression, the maut wins abune *(abin)* the meal? (1)
8. What is the meaning of the expression, miraculous fou *(foo)*? (1)
9. Supply the missing line in the following, taken from a Burns poem, for one point, and give the name of the poem for one point: (2)

    — — —, — — — —; (seven words)

Ae fareweel, and then, for ever!
10. Supply the missing line in the following, from a poem by Lady Nairne, for one point, and give the name of the poem for one point: (2)

    The Laird o' Cockpen, he's proud and he's great,

    — — — — — — — — — — — (eleven words)

SET F

1. What is the meaning of the adjective, paulie? (1)
2. What is the meaning of the noun, poulie *(poolie)*? (1)
3. What is the meaning of the proverb, "A proud hert in a puir breist has muckle dolour to dree"? (1)
4. What is the meaning of the proverb, "He that lippens to bodden ploughs, his land lies lea"? (1)
5. What are the Links of Forth in the following? (1)

    The lairdship of the bonny Links of Forth

    Is better than an earldom in the North.

6. What is the meaning of the sentence, Gie's your crack? (1)
7. What is the meaning of the phrase, the pokeshakins o the faimily? (1)
8. Supply the missing words (each dash stands for a letter) in the following lines for three points. Give the name of the poem for an extra point. (4)

>   D'ye mind the miller's dam,
>   When the frosty - - - - - - cam,
>   How we slid across the - - - - - -s' r - - -,
>   And made their gemm a sham?

9. Supply the missing words in the following lines for two points. Give the name of the poem for an extra point. Each dash stands for a letter. (3)

>   I wad wear thee in my - - - - -,
>   Lest my jewel I should - - - -.

10. Say whether the following statement is true or false. An extra point will be given for any relevant comment. (2)

>   The Luckenbooths in Edinburgh got its
>   name from the row of booths there that
>   could be locked up at night.

SET G

1. What is the meaning of the verb, to whummle? (1)
2. What is the meaning of the adjective, throuither? (1)
3. What is the meaning of the proverb, "Meisure twice and cut yince"? (1)
4. What is the meaning of the proverb, "Be aye the thing ye wad be caa'd"? (1)

5. Translate the following sentence into English to show you know the meaning of the phrases underlined: (2)

>He'll juist hae to gang through the mull like the lave o's.

6. Translate as for question 5: (2)

>When auld Jimmy was made the minister's man, he tint his gumption aathegither.

7. Say whether the following statement is true or false, for one point. An extra point will be given for any relevant comment. (2)

>The phrase, scot free, originates in the Scots' ancient ideals of freedom, liberty, and equality.

8. What is the meaning of the phrase, to play the plug? (1)

9. What is the meaning of the phrase, to get the road? (1)

10. In the following verse, give the meanings of the words underlined for four points, and name the poem from which the verse is taken for one point. (5)

>The cleanest corn that e'er was dight
>May hae some pyles o caff in,
>So ne'er a fellow-creature slight
>For randsome fits o daffin.

SET H

1. What sort of creature is a mawk? (1)
2. What sort of creature is a foumart *(foomart)*? (1)

3. What are the Daft Days? (1)
4. When is Mairtinmas; How did it get its name? (2)
5. What is the English for the Scots Christian name, Inga? (1)
6. What is the meaning of the proverb, "Ane does the skaith and anither gets the wyte"? (1)
7. What is the meaning of the proverb, "A sair flyter was never a guid fighter"? (1)
8. What was a lowpin-on-stane? (1)
9. Say whether the following statement is true or false, for one point. An extra point will be given for any relevant comment. (2)

> A mairriage lintel is a lintel stone of a door bearing the initials of a newly married couple who have set up house there.

10. In the following verse, give the meanings of the words underlined for four points, and name the poem from which the verse is taken for one point. (5)

> And aye he gied the tozy drab
> The tither skelpin kiss,
> While she held up her greedy gab,
> Juist like an aumous dish.

ANSWERS — WHA'LL BEAR THE GREE?

ANSWERS

WHA'LL BEAR THE GREE?

SET A

1. A working class friendly society or savings club.
2. To flatter, or wheedle.
3. Place someone in authority too early in life, and he'll shortly fall to the humblest of positions through misuse of his power.
4. Be careful not to betray yourself in the company of strangers.
5. Fleg means fright, claymores means large swords used by Scottish Highlanders; philabegs means kilts. The lines come from "Johnnie Cope" (by Adam Skirving).
6. The phrase means to speak with an affected English accent.
7. The phrase means genteel poverty.
8. The missing line is "Still gentler sister woman." It is from "Address to the Unco Guid."
9. The missing line is "Is ever wi my Jean." It is from "Of aa the Airts the Wind can Blaw."
10. False. A blin tam was a bundle of rags made up to pass as a child and carried by beggars to excite sympathy.

SET B

1. A cur; a mongrel.
2. Ill-bred; unbecoming; foolish.
3. A mercurial character is always greatly elated, or deeply despondent.
4. It's too late to take avoiding action when disaster is already upon one.
5. Dirlin means throbbing; halflin means adolescent or apprentice; spring means sprightly tune. The poem is "The Whistle" (by Charles Murray)
6. The phrase means all the same.
7. The phrase means wise in years.
8. The missing part-line is "(The shortening) winter day is

near a close." It is from "The Cotter's Saturday Night."
9. The missing line is "Looked asklent and unco skeich
   (skeich — guttural). It is from "Duncan Gray."
10. False. The title of the lament is "The Flowers of the
    Forest." The Flowers o' Edinburgh were either the smelly
    refuse thrown out into the streets, the lovely girls of
    Edinburgh, or a dance tune.

SET C

1. An odd-job man.
2. Firm; staunch.
3. To be too old a hand to be deluded with rubbish.
4. An old article (or person) keeps showing itself to be the
   worse for wear.
5. Agnes.
6. All of them.
7. Deeply ashamed.
8. Domineer over.
9. The missing words are spring; hale; grey.
10. True. It was used before barrows came into common use.
    It was also used for carrying peats from the moss.

SET D

1. The sorrel.
2. To confer; conspire.
3. Don't act rashly when you meet with a mishap.
4. You can't transform a thing, or person, into something
   which by nature it/he will never be.
5. But names will never hurt me.
6. Give someone a scolding.
7. Do a thing without preparation.
8. Albert.
9. The Union of Parliaments, 1707.
10. It's hardly in a body's power
    To keep at times frae being sour . . .
           From "Epistle to Davie"

SET E

1. To bargain; exchange.
2. A fiddler.
3. Look after your own people first.
4. To be worthy of good fortune, you must be willing to endure bad.
5. True. The clothes were steeped in lye of stale urine.
6. False. It was a biscuit, piece of cheese, or slice of christening cake, given to the first person met on the way to the christening. If the child was a girl, it was lucky to give to a man — if a boy, to a woman.
7. The drinker becomes drunk.
8. Very drunk.
9. Ae fond kiss, and then we sever . . .
        From "Ae fond Kiss"
10. His mind is taen up wi the things o' the state.
        From "The Laird o' Cockpen" (by Lady Nairne)

SET F

1. Weak; paralysed.
2. A louse.
3. If a proud man is also a poor one, he is likely to experience much unhappiness.
4. A man who relies on others' promises will never get anything done in life.
5. The Links of Forth is the land enclosed by the loops of the winding River Forth.
6. Tell me your news.
7. The last-born child in a family.
8. The missing words are winter; curlers'; rink. The name of the poem is "D'ye mind Langsyne?"
9. The missing words are bosom; tyne (meaning lose). The name of the poem is "Bonnie wee Thing" (by Robert Burns).
10. True. Located in the High Street, near St. Giles Kirk. Lucken means locked.

SET G

1. To capsize, overthrow.
2. Confused; unruly.
3. Think carefully before you act.
4. Always act the way you'd like folk to think you would act.
5. He'll just have to suffer the ordeals of life like the rest of us.
6. When old Jimmy became the church officer, he lost his commonsense completely.
7. False. It comes from the Old Norse word, skat, meaning tax. So it means tax free.
8. To play truant.
9. To be dismissed.
10. The word, dight, means winnowed; pyles means husks; caff means chaff; daffin means merriment. The verse comes from Burns's "Address to the Unco Guid."

SET H

1. A maggot.
2. A polecat.
3. The twelve days from Christmas Eve to 6th January.
4. 11th November. It is the festival of St. Martin of Tours.
5. Ingrid.
6. One does the harm, and another gets the blame.
7. One who scolds vehemently never fights well.
8. It was a block placed outstide churches and other public buildings to help ladies mount their horses.
9. True. The stone also bore the date of their marriage.
10. The word, tozy, means half drunk; drab means slattern; gab means mouth; aumous dish means alms dish. The verse comes from Burns's "Jolly Beggars."

GLOSSARY

Abe - Albert
abune - above
ae - one
aff-loof - extempore
agley - awry
aiblins - perhaps
aidle-dub - cesspool
Ailie - Alison
ain - own
airt - direction
argie-bargie - dispute
aulder - older
auld-farrant - wise beyond one's years
aumous - alms

Backgaun - languishing
baffs - house slippers
baggie - belly
bane - bone
bannet - bonnet
barm - yeast
bauchle - to shuffle; old, feeble person
baudrons - cat
baukie bird - bat
bausy - big and fat
bawbee - halfpenny
bawsent - white-streaked
Beenie - Robina
begowk - deceive
begrutten - stained with tears
beil - fester
Beltane - 1st May, quarter day

belyve - soon; presently
benmaist - innermost
bethankit - grace after meal
bien - affluent; cosy
big - build
billies - companions; fellows
binkie - little chest
birkie - alert; animated
birl - rotate
birsle - broil; roast
bizzum - broomstick; loose woman
black affrontit - thoroughly ashamed
blackfit - lovers' go-between
blate - timid
blecknin - boot polish
blellum - silly, talkative person
bletherin - talkative
blin - blind
blue dykie - hedge sparrow
bocht - bought
bodden - promised
bodle - small coin
boke - gush forth
bore - recess
boss - empty
bouat - hand lantern
bou-houcht - bandy-legged
bouk - bulk; size

boukin	- annual washing by steeping in lye of urine	canny	- cautious
		canty	- comfortable; merry
bowf	- bark	careous	- curious
bowlie	- bow-legged	carnaptious	- crabbed
brace	- mantleshelf	cauld	- cold
braisant	- bold; insolent	caurry-fistit	- left-handed
brammle	- bramble	causey	- cobbled street
braws	- best clothes	caw	- drive
brecham	- horse collar	champ	- mash; pound
bree	- liquid; gravy	channer	- complain; fret
breeks	- trousers	chapman	- pedlar
brierd	- germinate	chawsome	- disappointing
brek	- break	chitter	- shiver
brent	- smooth	chitterin bite	- food taken after bathing
brock	- badger		
brose	- porridge	chynge	- change
brosie	- coarse; stout	claes	- clothes
broukit	- soiled	claggy	- sticky
bruckle	- brittle	claivers	- tittle-tattle
bubblyjock	- turkey	clamjamfry	- mob; rabble
bucht	- sheepfold	clarty	- dirty; messy
bumclock	flying beetle	clashbag	- a gossip
bunemaist	- topmost	clatchy	- muddy
Buntie	- Margaret	claut	- scraper
burnie	- small stream	cleik	- crook; hook
busk	- clothe; make ready	cleuch	- crag; coal pit
		clinty	- flinty; stony
but-and-ben	- two-roomed cottage	clockin	- broody
		clour	- beat; strike
byde	- stay	clout/cloot	- cloth
		clowt	- strike; slap
Ca'	- call	clug	- log of wood; wooden shoe
caff	- chaff		
callan	- boy	clype	- tell-tale
caller	- cool; fresh	cockie-leekie	- leek and chicken soup
cam	- came		
camsteerie	- unruly	coddled aipples	- roasted apples
cangle	- quibble		

cog	- bowl	dee	- die
collieshangie	- dispute; brawl	deil	- devil
coom	- soot	deoch-an-dorus	- stirrup cup; parting drink
cou/coo	- cow	dicht	- wipe
coorie	- bend; cower	diffy	- dull; stupid
corbies	- ravens	ding	- dash down; surpass
cowp	- overturn		
cowt	- colt	dinna	- do not
crack	- talk	dirlin	- throbbing
craig	- neck; throat	Dod	- George
cranreuch	- hoarfrost	donnert	- stupid
crawsteps	- steps on house gable	doo	- dove
		douce	- decorous; grave
creepie-stool	- three-legged stool; church stool of repentance		
		douk/dook	- bathe; dip
		dour	- stubborn
		dourles	- sulks
creish	- grease	dowf	- gloomy; spiritless
crichle	- wheezy throat irritation		
		dowie	- dejected
		dowp	- backside
croun	- crown	drappie	- small drop
crouse	- cheerful; jaunty	dree	- endure
		dreip	- drip
crummock	- staff with crook for handle	drouk/drook	- drench
		droun/droon	- drown
		drouthy	- thirsty
cuif/coof	- fool; simpleton	drucken	- drunk
		drummly	- muddy
cundy	- conduit; drain	dub	- pond; bog
		dwyne	- wane; decline in health
curfuffle	- disorder; excitement		
cushie doo	- wood-pigeon	Eck	- Alexander
cutty-cley	- short stemmed clay pipe	ee	- eye
		een	- eyes
		Effie	- Euphemia
		eldritch	- frightful; hideous
Dandie	- Andrew		
deave	- deafen; bore	ettle	- intend

evendoun	- outright	gallowses	- man's braces
		gam-teetht	- having lapping teeth
Fain	- eager; eagerly		
fairin	- deserts	gang	- go
fashed	- bothered	gar	- cause; make
fashous	- troublesome	gash	- animated; clever
faurer	- farther		
fecht	- fight	gaun	- going
feckless	- incompetent	gear	- effects; money
fidged	- fidgeted		
fitpad	- footpath	gee/jee	- stir
flauchter	- flutter	gemm	- game
flee	- fly	geylies	- rather
fleg	- fright	Gibbie	- Gilbert
fleich	- flatter; wheedle	gie	- give
		girnin	- complaining
flicher	- flutter	girr	- hoop
flicht	- flight	Girzie	- Griselda
flichter-lichtie	- unstable person	glaury	- muddy
		gleg	- alert; nimble
flet	- plate	glunch	- frown; sulk
flyter	- scolder	goldie	- goldfinch
forby	- besides	gomeril	- stupid person
forfochen	- exhausted	gorlin	- fledgling
forrit	- forward	gowd	- gold
fou	- full	gowdspink	- goldfinch
foumart	- polecat	gowk	- fool
fozie	- flabby; spongy	graip	- manure fork
		green	- lawn
frae	- from	greit/greet	- weep
fremmit	- strange	growes	- grows
fuggie-toddler	- a small yellow bee	grumph	- grunt
		guddle	- grope with hands
fushionless	- dull; tasteless		
fykie	- fussy; exacting	guid	- good
		guidwillie	- cordial
		gumption	- intelligence
Gab	- mouth		
gaen	- gone	Habbie	- Albert
gallivant	- gad about	hae	- have
gallus	- daring; rash	haffits	- temples

hairst	- harvest	jawbox	- kitchen sink
haisert	- half dried off	jennie-meggie	- cranefly
haivers	- nonsense	joug	- jug
halflin	- adolescent	jouk	- dodge
hame	- home		
handsel	- celebrate with a gift	Kail	- soup
harns	- brains	keekin-gless	- mirror
haud	- hold	kenspeckle	- prominent
haun	- hand	kent	- knew
hause	- gullet; neck	Kirstie	- Christina
heather-bleat	- snipe	kist	- chest; box
heich	- high	kitchen	- relish
heid	- head	kittle	- tickle
het	- heated	knaggie	- bony
heuk	- hook; sickle	kytes	- stomachs
hippit	- lamed with thigh strain		
hizzie	- hussy	Ladle	- church collection box
hoch	- lower thigh		
hotched	- fidgeted	laich	- low
houlet	- owl	laird	- landowner
howe-backit	- hollow-backed	laith	- loath
		lane, your lane	- you alone
humph	- hump	lang	- long
humplock	- hillock	langsyne	- long ago
hurdies	- buttocks	lap	- leapt
hurkle-bane	- hip bone	lappert	- curdled
hushion	- stocking with foot worn away	lauch	- laugh
		laverock	- lark
		lea	- leave
		lea	- unploughed
Ilka	- each; every	leal	- faithful
Inga	- Ingrid	Leebie	- Elizabeth
ingle	- fire	leerie	- lamplighter
		lees	- lies
Jalouse	- conjecture; suspect	leeve	- live
		Leezie	- Elizabeth
jaud	- jade; perverse woman	leister	- three-pronged fish spear
jaups	- splashes		

let on	- divulge	maskin pot	- teapot
lig	- lie	maun	- must
link	- stride; trip lightly	mawk	- maggot
		mealy-mou'd	- plausible
links	- land enclosed by river windings	meir	- mare
		mell	- mallet
		mennen	- minnow
lippen	- trust; rely on	merle	- blackbird
loaning	- lane	merse	- flat rich ground by river
loun/loon	- fellow; rascal		
lout	- stoop; curtsy		
lowse	- loosen	mey	- hawthorn flower
lowsin time	- time for stopping work for the day		
		midden	- dunghill
		mim-mou'd	- prim
		Minnie	- Mary, Marion
lowe	- flame	Mirren	- Marion
lowp	- leap	monie	- many
lowpin-on-stane	- stone block to assist rider to mount horse	mou	- mouth
		mowdie	- mole
		muckle	- much
		Nan	- Agnes; Ann
Lowrie	- Lawrence	Nansie	- Agnes
lug	- ear	nappie	- ale; beer
luggies	- bowls	near-the-bit	-miserly
luif/loof	- palm of hand	neb	- nose
lum hat	- top hat	neips	- turnips
lyart	- grey; variegated	nesh	- tender; sensitive
		nickietams	- trouser leg straps
Mailie	- Mollie		
mair	- more	nieve	- fist
Mamie	- Jemima or Marion	niffer	- bargain; exchange
Mairtinmas	- 11th November, feast of St Martin	nipscart	- miser
		noddle	- head
		norie	- whim
		nyaff	- contempible person
manawdge	- neighbours' friendly society		
		Ocht	- aught

oo	- wool	pyke	- pick
ower	- over		
owsen	- oxen	Quaich	- shallow two-handled drinking cup
oxter	- armpit		
		quey	- heifer
Parritch	- porridge	quine	- girl; hussy
paulie	- weak; paralysed		
pawmie	- stroke with strap	Rax	- stretch
		reamed	- effervesced
peeli-wallie	- sickly; delicate	redd	- clean up
		reiky	- smoky
peenie	- pinafore	richt	- right
peerie	- spinning top	rickle	- loose pile
peevers	- hopscotch	rieve	- rend; rip
penny buff	- school primer	rip	- handful of corn
pennie- geggie	- travelling show		
		rockin	- gathering of women to spin and gossip
penny jo	- prostitute		
penny waddin	- wedding at which guests paid to get in		
		rodden tree	- rowan tree
penny wheep	- weak ale	rousty	- rusty
perjink	- fastidious	rowe	- roll
peys	- pays	runkle	- wrinkle; crease
Phemie	- Euphemia		
philabegs	- kilts		
pinkie	- little finger	Sain	- bless
pirn	- bobbin	sair	- sore
pit	- put	sall	- shall
plowter	- potter/splash about	sark	- shirt
		sarkin	-wood roof lining
pokeshakins	- last-born member of family		
		saut	- salt
		scaffie	- scavenger
poulie	- louse	scrieve	- write
pourie	- cream jug	sea-maw	- seagull
pow	- head	seck	- sack
preen	- pin	semmit	- vest; under-shirt
preencod	- pin-cushion		
puir	- poor	shairn	- cow dung

shauchle	- shuffle; shamble	sou/soo	- a sow
shears	scissors	souch/sooch	- sigh
shilpit	- puny; shrunken	soups	- sweeps
		sourock	- the sorrel
sheuch	- ditch	sowens	- pudding of oat husks
shoon	- shoes	speir	- ask
sib	- akin	speug	- sparrow
Sibbie	- Isabella	spring	- a sprightly tune
sic	- such		
siccar	- sure; certain	spirlie	- slender
siller	- silver; money	spune	- spoon
Simie	- Simon	spurtle	- porridge stirrer
skaith	- injury		
skail	- spill	stang	- stung
skailin time	- time for closing	stang	- a pole
		steik/steek	- stitch
skeily	- skilful	steirin	- mischievous
skelf	- sliver	steive	- steady; staunch
skellum	- rogue		
skelpit	- slapped	stirk	- bullock
skinkin ware	- watery soup	stook	- group of sheaves set up to dry
skirl-i-the-pan	- oatmeal and onion fry		
slaiger	- besmear	stookie	- stucco
slaistert	- smeared	stot	- bounce
slee	- sly	stour	- dust
sleekit	- hypocritical; sly	stovies	- potatoes stewed with onions
sleepie-mannie	- speck in the eye		
		straucht	- straight
sliddery	- slippery	sune	- soon
smirr	- drizzle	swatch	- sample
smit	- infect	swats	- ale
snaw	- snow	swee	- pivot for suspending pot over fire
sneck	- bolt; latch		
sned	- lop off		
snell	- cold; sharp	sweirt	- loath
snicker	- titter	syne	- rinse
snood	- hair ribbon		
soo	- ache	Taigle	- hinder

tak	- take		with labour
tam-o-shanter	- cap with	trewan	- trowel
	broad, flat	trews	- tartan tousers
	top and	trowe	- trundle
	pompom	trystist	- bespoken;
tappit hen	- decanter		invited
	topped with	tuim	- empty
	hen's comb	tyauve/chauve	- struggle
tattie-beetle	- potato	tyke	- dog
	masher	tyne	- lose
tattie-ploum	- fruit on		
	potato plant	Unco	- strange;
	after flower		extremely
tatties-'n-dab	- potatoes and	usquebae	- whisky
	salt		
tawse	- teacher's	Vieve	- lively; vivid
	strap		
Teenie	- Christina	Wad	- wager
tent	- notice; listen	wae	- woe; woeful
	to	waff	- puff
teuch	- tough	wale	- select
thairm	- catgut; fiddle	walie	- ample; large
	string	wally-dug	- china dog
thairm-scraper	- fiddler	wame	- stomach
theik/theek	- thatch	wat	- wet
thocht	- thought	wather	- bad weather
tholin	- enduring	waucht	- deep draught
thrapple	- throat		of liquor
thraw	- twist	wede	- withered
thrawn	- stubborn	weit/weet	- wet
threip	- assert	whang	- thong
	dogmatically	wheeple	- whistle
Tib	- Elizabeth	whigmaleeries	- whims
tippenny	- small beer	whussles	- whistles
tocher	- purse; dowry	whyles	- sometimes
toddle	- saunter	winna	- will not
tosh	- tidy	winnock	- window
toun	- town	wizzened	- shrunken
tozie	- half drunk	worset	- wool
traik	- trudge	wyce	- wise
trauchled	- overburdened	wyte	- blame

Yammer	- complain
yella yite	- yellow hammer
yestreen	- yesterday evening
yeuk	- itch
yin	- one
yird	- earth
yowes	- ewes